White BUTTERFLY

EDITION 1.0

Nwike Ebuka Godwin

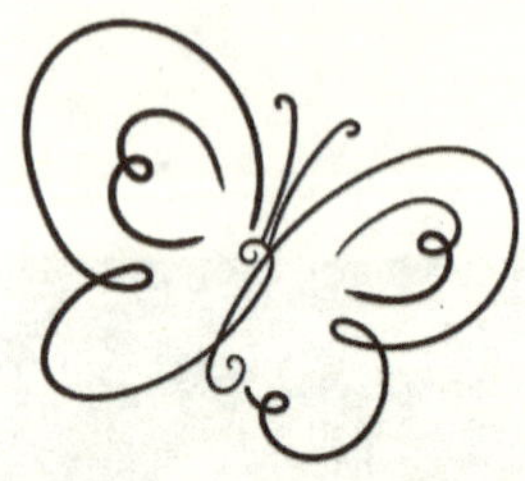

NATIONAL LIBRARY OF NIGERIA CATALOGUING-IN-PUBLICATION DATA

White Butterfly
GODWIN, Nwike Ebuka,
1. Christian poetry, Nigerian (English)
2. Nigerian poetry (English)
I. Title

PR1195.C48 G591 2024 821.92
ISBN: 978-978-62019-6-2 (pbk) AACR2

White Butterfly (Edition 1.0)

ISBN: 978-978-62019-6-2

Published and printed by:

Pen-Impact Writing and Publishing Enterprise
16 Adedoyin Rhodes-Vivour Close, Asokoro,
Abuja, FCT, Nigeria
Website: www.pen-impact.com
Email: info@pen-impact.com
Tel: +234 701 990 4999

Table of Contents

Not that way

Foreword

The anthology **White Butterfly** contains Godly poems that give you poems to inspire, motivate, build your relationships, have a good relationship with God, help you realise God's light and love, and provide Christians with Godly poetry. The content of each poem is powerful and inspiring. Each poem is different from the other but interwoven with each other. Being the first of my publication, this is my gift to the world. **White Butterfly** is filled with so many virtues. So feel the vibe and enjoy as you read.

Acknowledgements

The Grace of God has made it possible for this book to come to life. I return all glory to Him. I'm so grateful to God for my family. Their prayer and support helped me so much. First, my mum (Nwike Sweet Omonigo), so daring, your prayers for me each day made me strong. Now you've gone to be with the Lord- April 2024, but you left another rare gem in this world. You pushed me to grow and be better, to improve more; your prayers and encouragement were not in vain, and I'm growing stronger. To my brother Nwike Chibuike, you have been very helpful in reading my poems all the way and letting me know those little errors I need to correct, and in helping me with some projects and digital assistance I needed in tech and others; thank you. I also want to appreciate my sister (Nwike Adaeze) for her support; thank you for assisting me. To my colleague and co-teacher, Miss Sandra, I appreciate your efforts in helping me type the contents of these poems. I also appreciate my second mum, my mum's twin sister (Mrs Ruth Oyedele); you have been really encouraging. Thank you so much for all the love and support that pushed us to chase big dreams.

I appreciate all those who featured in a poem, Theophilus (Theophy IP), Nicky Inks (Collins Otuoze Thomas). Thank you so much.

I also want to express my appreciation to my online audience on different social media platforms for their support and follow. Thank you.

And also to my friends, families, and church leaders, who I didn't mention but who have encouraged me and pushed me to be better in one way or the other, I say thank you, thank you so much for everything.

Lastly, I appreciate Pen-impact Writing and Publishing Enterprise for their services in publishing this book; thank you.

Dedication

In loving memory, this book is dedicated to my loving mum (Nwike Sweet Omonigo). A great woman of virtues.

WHAT DO YOU SEE?

1. Reflection

The reflective waves of reflection is reflection,
It holds the personality of the reflected. Reflection shows,
Reflection reflects,
It is unimaginary, for the reality fact of reflection,
Is that it shows who you are.
Reflection, reflection,
Who are you when reflected?
Does your life point others to Christ?
Do people see your life with meaning?
Does God trust you with that life?
Reflection is only reflection, but it's true.
Who you are deep down,
Is reflected to others daily as you live.

2. Empty

Empty bottles, cans and tins
Still, they think
But cannot think.
Shows is only what they show,

Yet they think
But got no mint.
If you try to search empty things,
You'll never find anything,
Empty things, empty things.

3. Memories

I have thought of a thought
It was a "thinking thought"
I have dreamt of a dream
It wasn't dreaming dreams
They were memories.

4. Beyond the horizon

Beyond the horizon,
There is more.
If you look far,
You'll find the untold stories.
Beyond the horizon,
There's something more amazing.
The most amazing thing you'll find is true love.
Beyond the horizon,
There are silly tricks it does.
The fog, the dew and dust,
Creates some unclear views.
Beyond the horizon,
If you look deep,
You'll truly find the treasure island you seek.
Beyond the horizon,
There is that which you can call home.
It awaits you,
Just beyond the horizon.

5. Zero - Hero

I'm tired of coming back to zero,
Cause I want to be a hero,
And zero is not a hero.
Hypocrisy makes us a big zero,
Like a bent number one,
And that's not a hero.
Failure has many zeros,
But success has something than zero,
And this makes a hero.
If you want to become a hero,
Start with God to erase the zeros,
So you can have a clean path to be a hero.
Many want to count millions with many zeros,
But one having hate and millions without God is even a zero.
God in us through Christ Jesus makes us a hero.
Don't zero Him out of your life.
For only He makes us the best heroes.

6. Laying on the bed

I lay on my bed,
And looked into the ceiling,
And my mind went to the past events of the day.
I thought and imagined,
And as I imagined,
I felt joyful to have achieved the day.
For then, the comfort of my bed made me fast asleep,
Leading my imagination to the sweetest dream of the night.

7. Blinded sight

"The gift that dies is the dead gift in time."
How can the blind lead the blind?
Is that not 'the death line' that traps a life?

Blinded sight - seeing light yet believing the dark.
In real life the blind is leading the blind.
Both are 'walking lies,' believing they're doing right.
Open your eyes, indeed, and see the light.
Say not now but now! for each timeline is timed.
In this life, follow not the blind-leading-blinds
Such are blinded sight, believers of lies, walking in the dark.
So choose your path - walk in the light,
Believe God for your life - HE makes all things bright.

8. Catching Beauty

Purity, indeed, is the sacred beauty,
Though many may not see it,
But those who have seen it,
Knows that within, it's filled with true beauty.
Feelings is not the catching beauty,
It fades, it changes, and doesn't stay.
But within lies purity in a cleansed heart,
And this is the 'catching beauty' that dims not in life.

9. Writing Gift

I can't stop writing
I can't stop writing
If I stop, I am dead
For it is the gift given of God.
My first poem written on the 1st of December 2015

10. Bubbles

Bubbling bubbles,
It ain't gonna bubble itself.
You have got to blow the bubbles,
And let it float away,
And in many ways, it will go,

In several directions, it will float.
But the bubbled bubbles did not blow itself,
It floated away,
Because you blew the "bubbles".

GOD IS GOOD

1. Rainbow

Rainbow's bow of
Sunshine lights,
How beautiful are thy colour
that shines so bright.
Rainbow colours
Here and there,
God's promised proof
that truly He cares.

2. Full moon

Full moon it was,
Bright light it shone,
Up high it stood,
Reflecting sun rays downward.
The full moon was good,
It never shone at noon,
But waited till noon had passed,
And the blue turned dark.
Full moon, full moon,

28 days for its complete cycle,
For it to become a big circle,
Shining bright over the Earth's circle.

3. Sky Dream

He sat on a wooden chair,
And thought of his wonders.
Above the tree into the sky,
He looked and wondered.
What does my future hold?
What is the unknown that I need to know?
What is the dream God has for my life?
As he looked steadfastly into the sky,
He saw an airplane and realised the answer to his long-searched desire,
Go higher, sky dream.

4. Blessed Morning

Rising early in the morning,
I saw the puddles of last night's rain.
Rising early in the morning,
And seeing so much at peace,
Makes my heart feel at peace.
Rising early in the morning to seek God,
Is a perfect time to choose.
Rising early, and the morning stars
Are just morning to you.
Rising early and the moon smiles at you,
Makes a good difference to your soul.
For what a blessed morning,
To simply have peace and joy.

5. The Key of Thy Life

The key of thy life, for thy life,
Is never determined by thy past.
A key shutteth, a key openeth,
A key is the key, for there is none other to open rightly the door.
The key of thy life is in God,
For when we hope in Him,
He gives us the key of life,
Christ Jesus, His Son.

6. My Favourite Superhero

God's love is sure,
At the cross, it shone,
The bright Gospel light of God,
- Christ Jesus, His son.
God's love is pure,
His promises fail not,
His love is strong,
For surely, when we call on Him,
He never fails to pick up the call.
Too long, the world thought,
A hero from God may take too long.
But then, He sent His only Son,
The surest superhero to save this sinful world.

7. Godly Sense And Wisdom

Wisdom is the principal thing,
With it, you will find good gifts.
Sense is a powerful tool,
All who use it never regret its good.
Sense is very intense,
Hence, in all intents,
Use godly sense,

So that without pretence,
You can avoid all unrighteousness.

8. Peace Within

There is peace within,
Because I've found something peaceful.
There is a springing well of Joy,
Because I'm pulled out of a well.
There is peace within,
Because my life has been sweetened.
There is all of peace in my heart,
Because I have the Prince of Peace - Jesus

9. Sacrifice

HE gave Him all for thee,
Christ's death was all for thee,
To the cross, He went for you,
And became the sacrifice just for thee.
Why then has thou not yielded to Him?
His whole life He gave for you and me,
A ransom for the world, chosen to be,
He became the sacrifice to set us free from sin.

10. Thank you Lord

Thank you, Lord, for everything,
Thank you, Lord, for every day.
Thank you, Lord, every now and then,
Thank you, Lord, Thank you, Lord.
Thank you, Lord, for everything,
Thank you, Lord, for each new day.
Many things have come and gone,
Thank you so much for the things you've done.
Thank you, Lord, for everything,

Each new bliss brings thankful things,
Even in bad times, you're still there,
Thank you, Lord, for every good you have done.

BEAMS OF HOPE

1. Two boys

Two boys great,
Two boys strong,
Two boys, very able,
Two boys, two boys.......
Two boys who will take up destiny,
And who will stand for God firmly,
Always moving forward,
Two boys, two boys.......

>>> **Dedicated to my students Ose & Praise Daniels**

2. Twilight

Twilight beams
Of sunlight rays,
Soft and tender
Calm you are.
The setting sun
And the rising sun,
Calls to thee

Below the horizon.
Twilight sky
I got back home,
Was what I saw
When it was setting sun.

3. Silver Lining

Silver lining, silver lining,
Over the edge, towards the end,
There is a bright side,
Silver lining, silver lining.
His hope was high,
His mind was set,
His goal was aimed,
Silver lining, silver lining.

4. Sometimes

Sometimes we wanna go, sometimes we wanna stay.
Sometimes it's all blue, sometimes it's all plain.
Sometimes we want to go home,
Other times, we might need to leave home.
Sometimes it's scary, but we have to take courage.
Sometimes it's all noisy, sometimes it's quiet.
Sometimes it's hard; sometimes, it's easy.
Sometimes we wanna run, other times we wanna walk.
Sometimes it's rosy, sometimes it's not fine,
Sometimes, sometimes,
All I can say is, everything got it's time for the 'SOME'.

5. All Seems Well

I looked out the window,
To find a boy who fell off an old bike.
His fall brought a cut,

But someone around,
Ran towards the injured boy,
To clean his wound,
To assist and aid him,
Then I said to myself - All seems well.

6. Sunshine

Now it has rained,
Sunshine come.
Bloom everywhere with light,
So all will know.
Stay not under the clouds,
But clear in the sky.
Make the cold go away,
And make everywhere warm.

7. Obedience

Obedience comes from the heart,
Obedience of the heart with the mind,
There is no wrong motive behind thy response,
For it is an immediate answer to the call.
Obedience brings the greatest,
Obedience is a choice, it slacks not,
Obedience is a pillar in the foundation of life,
Obedience will surely obey.

8. Medicine

Healing beams, healing rays of light,
Awakened from sleep, awakened my heart to love.
Healing beams, healing light and love,
Medicine you are, that brings cure to a dying soul.
Healing beams, healing rays of light,
God's love found me, God's love saved me.

Its healing beams has healed me,
Sweet forgiveness, sweet medicine for the soul.

9. Little

When the little is much,
It's because of the great in the little.
When the great is little,
It's because the little is not great.
When you see the little ones,
Around the great ones,
It's because the little seeks to be great.
And when the little truly is great,
It becomes greater because of more little greatness,
Added timely to it.

10. Music Again

Deep down within the soul,
Is where the pains and aches are felt.
Music, good music helps soothe it away,
Music again, sweet music for the soul.
Hoping again, hoping to find love again,
Music will help ease the pain,
And make the "rain gaze",
Sweet music, sweet music for the soul.

THEY DON'T KNOW

1. Stones

Stones they did hold,
To wound Him whole,
That was sent to save their soul.
They took to Him the adulterous woman,
Master, shall we cast the stones? They inquired.
He that is without 'sins', let him first cast a stone.
Stones of no worth you do hold,
While you reject the cornerstone,
Remove ye the stone, cast ye away the stones.

2. Rhymes

Who can stew the pure dew?
Who can barbecue the moon?
Two boo cannot rescue moo,
A few dew, a new blue.
The pursuit was not for some cool tools,
But was to ensure Cue's pure treasure cube,
Was not wooed from Sue.
They were in the queue since noon,
Still, they couldn't rescue their nephew's new pews.
They argued a few times,

Because they didn't pay their dues.
Grandpa, how did Coo know?
Well, that's part of the story too.
Coo read the news
And so he secured the goods.
Well, that's all for the night,
That's all the rhymes,
Goodnight Boo.

3. Bruce

Pascal Bruce was his name,
Blaise Blues was his brother.
He rode on his cruise,
But wasn't like one of those junk fools.
If he was to use his goods,
He was careful not to lose his boots.
And even his foods,
Were like some precious goods.
"When he zooms, he doesn't drones".
Who is he?
His name is Bruce.

4. Running Silas

Running, where are you running to Silas?
Give your soul to God, and let Him be for you.
Running Silas! When will you heed and turn to God?
So you can stop this unprofitable race.
Art thou a Jonah? You can run but cannot hide - God is everywhere.
Come seek refuge,
Look to the future, there is no end to thy dangerous run.
Run to God, run to Him, and He will surely be for you.

5. Sinking

Sinking zinc,
It was all a sink.
Unsinkable steel,
Still couldn't defeat
the sink.
The sink, the zinc,
The unsinkable zinc,
Was also part of the sink.
All was a sink,
Sinking zinc...........
Sinking steel............

6. Does it worth it?

Does it matter in matters?
Is it worth the pain?
Many things are struggled for worthlessly,
They seek it out blindly without insight.
Does it worth it? Is it worthy?
Seek to do the matters that matter,
For that is the worth that is worthwhile.
God's true plan is worthy and true,
Yes, it is worth it, the worth is true.

7. The day I wrestled peace

Truth be told, I wasn't me;
Deep down, I knew because it wasn't real.
Faked it too long, but still, it wouldn't do;
And now truths are unfolding.
I just wanted to be true,
But I wrestled too long with the truth,
But now I cease from those deeds,
To find peace and be at peace.

8. Hidden tears

Still unknown - is the tears they don't know,
Bleeding me, my mind is losing me.
Thinking deep, I hope I don't lose me,
For within me, there are hidden tears untold.
The stress of the 'living reals ' - is real,
I hope I cope, I pray I don't lose the zeal- the zeal of hope,
My emotions have become waving motions,
In this I see not me, but hidden tears only.

9. Too busy to see

You don't see it,
You don't want to see it,
So why should I force you to see it?
I went "beyond the brooks" for you so you could believe me,
So you could see it, but you never did!
I don't know if it's attention you seek,
But what I know is this,
you're "too busy to see".

10. Chasing the bag

I chased the bag, and for real, it was hard.
I lost my mind, ignored family, because I wanted it so bad.
The bag itself is not bad, but there's more to life;
And when you do not see the others, you will think the bag is life.
You said you're chasing the bag -
Have you found it in thy chase?
The bag will make you keep on chasing it,
Until it feels as if you are being chased.
So why not find something purposely to do,
And let the 'bag' find you.

LOVE AND PAIN

1. Turtledoves

Two turtledoves of love,
Two turtledoves were in love.
Two pieces that got so fixed,
Two pieces forever fixed.
Two turtledoves were in love;
Two turtledoves, two turtledoves,
Two turtledoves forever in love.

2. Sorrow not

"The cry for the day,
That the night should end",
Is close to the end.
For the night's call is set,
To bring daylight that has no end,
Oh dear child, sorrow not.
Take heart and be strong,
For the Lord is coming,
And in His light so bright,
The dark night is conquered,

Oh dear child, sorrow not.

3. Roses

Roses, falling down,
Love, melting away,
Shows the unloved story.
Rose bliss that brings peace,
Is found in pure love of sweet dreams.
Roses…………, Roses……………
They are so pleasant when shared with the right heart.

4. Brotherhood

Brotherhood, under the hood of brothers can you find brotherhood.
Brotherhood is not in having many brothers,
But in creating the hood for the brothers.
There is a mood that maintains the hood of brothers,
The brotherhood is maintained in love.
There are many other hoods,
And these other hoods like the neighbourhood, sisterhood, and the motherhood;
And fatherhood and childhood, all got some hoods.
But in all these other hoods,
There must be the brotherhood, the
oneness or else it becomes some falsehood.
Take the mood for the hood,
Which is the love for the hood,
And keep the brotherhood.

5. Blues

Blue river brought your blue boots to me.
I went straight home under the blue moon.
As I walked on,

I pondered on the boots of blue.
I came to Buckingham,
And right across me was a beautiful damsel,
In clothes of pure blue but on barefoot.
And I said to myself,
This must be her blues.

6. Once upon a time

Once upon a time, within time,
There was a time I would run to her,
Once upon a time....
Once upon a time, only once daily,
But more than once weekly,
Do I leave for her a rose flower,
Once upon a time.....
Once upon a time,
It is more than that time,
I still love her to this time,
Once upon a time.

7. The story of the "Fake Love"

I wanna love she said,
But you don't wanna hold me?
Isn't that fake love?
I thought you'll be there,
I came running,
But you were never there.
Your actions have voiced itself,
that you will not be there,
And truly, you were never there.
I trusted you and cared,
You took all my money and didn't care.
And you want me to still care?

I was blinded not to see,
And I truly loved you from deep within;
But all you gave me was fake from within.
I wanted to make you my world, show you where I came from,
But you broke your word,
And now I feel like I need a sword.
Not to kill,
But to wield it to shun the evil ones,
Cause I'm tired of fake love.
You said we're just friends,
Then why did you stay too long to leave?
Your love for me was fake!
I felt so hurt,
And I did cry,
But I didn't die, and so I'll rise.
You tell me grown-up men don't cry,
If tears were love,
At least my part wasn't fake.
I don't wanna hate,
And so I'll take the lessons and learn from the mistakes;
And move on with life to find true love.
Dear Lord, help me in this life,
As I move on to find true love,
Help me that it'll never be fake.

8. Forgetting the pains

When we live in our yesterday,
We live in the pains thereof.
When we choose to forget and forgive the past,
We become free from the pains.
The past and its pains are one,
Making the mind and heart blurred to see the future.
The pains, oh the pains,
Can never benefit our life.

The pains make us in pain,
And there is no other way,
Our life can be sweetened,
Except we 'forget' the pains.

9. Bitter pains

Bitter pains ache longer than headaches,
Headache has its pains but is less than bitter pains.
Bitter pain breaks, it drains,
It strains, and stays like 'mental blake'.
Bitter pains make you wish the wishing wish,
The wishing wish to reverse the pains, to feel no pain;
To go back in time and reverse the event!
That brought the bitter pains.
Aching aches - to whom shall I tell the deep things of these pains?
To few I tried but it wouldn't do.
Then to Christ, I went, my saviour and friend,
HE saved me, and forgave me, and healed me of my bitter pains.

10. When I find her

When I find her,
I will know and understand.
When I find her,
My very heart, in God's lead, will see.
When I find her,
My sweet dream of her in my heart will understand.
When I find her,
She'll be the one truly meant for me.

DESTINY AND I

1. Go!

Going gets us to our goal,
Delaying doesn't make us go,
It hinders the goal.
You have got to go!
For you to reach your goals,
You have to GO!

2. Walking tall

You need to walk up tall,
Leave all fears and go on up,
Stand up firm and hold it right,
Walking tall............
Walking tall, walking tall....
It is not about your height,
Stand upright, take it right,
See the light and walk up tall.
Now you see the light,
Rise up in it's might,
Leave thy fears, make it right,
Walking tall............

3. Home

I wanna go home, said Brooks;
Why.............? I don't just feel at home.
Where is Home?
Home can be anywhere.
It is not just the house,
Home is love, a place of love.
Home is peace,
Home is joy, Home is happiness,
Home gives you hope.
Home is priceless and never worthless,
Home is gorgeous.
Home is nice, it is beautiful.
Home can be handsome too,
If it's never left empty and so lonely.
Home can be cold,
If you fail to turn up the 'heat'.
Home sweet Home,
God's love in the home sweetens any home.
** Where is Home? Home is never far away when there is love.

4. Race

Race for it,
At the sound of the hit, go for it.
I remember a story, how the hare lost the race;
It lost its focus, it lost first place.
Stay focused to win in the race,
Avoid it on-coming distractions,
So as to win the game.
Stay on it, race for it, and go for it.
The race that is perfect starts with God and ends with God.
Put " HIM" in your "Race".

5. Purpose

Redefined and purposed,
I had to lose all to find one.
Finding life's meaning,
The way of truth I had to take.
I was vague for too long,
So unclear on how to be strong;
But now, I see the wrongs,
I've seen what I've done wrong.
Money was not the purpose,
Our doings were the purpose,
Doing God's will gave purpose,
Cause life's true meaning is found in His purpose.

6. Dreams

Dreams got its ways of fulfilment.
Dreams are big, but many times, we limit the dreams.
Dreams, some dreams are fantasy, others are real.
Take the dream that God has for thee,
Never let it go, but believe.
Take the song of good destiny He has planned,
Never let it go, but believe.
Take the promise of the dream to fulfil your dreams,
Never let it go, but pray and believe.

7. Iwaju

Into the unknown with what we know,
We shall arrive into what shall be known.
Fear is not what we should hold, but to be BOLD,
So, into the future, we will go, for therein lies the greatest gold—
Iwaju.
In the fear of danger, we will not fear danger,
For what we seek is greater, greater than any other.

So with great courage, we will go, fighting to conquer enemies or foes,
With strength from above, we will not fold—Iwaju

8. Trees on a hill

Trees on a hill,
Life is but a dream.
If you seek out the real deals,
You'll find out what is real.
Trees on a hill,
Different scenes you will see.
The things of ancient deeds,
And memories are what you will see.
Trees on a hill,
Life ain't a movie scene.
The real life is what you will see,
As you journey through these "hills".
Trees on a hill,
Only the patient will win.
Yes! "The race is not a race unless you race",
But what's your direction? What is your dream?
Focus on the dream,
"And not on the trees".
Focus on the seeds,
As you journey through these hills.
Life comes with its own ills,
But only those with skills will win.
The tree is on the hill,
What is your seed? What is your dream?
Trees on a hill,
They are green and evergreen.
If you seek out what is real,
You will find the real deals.
Trees on a hill,

Planets, but only one has trees.
What do you see?
Where are your seeds? What is your dream?

9. Brief Life

What a short life!
It is so brief,
Seemingly nothing but truly full of something.
What a brief life!
What is life?
It is only meaningful when we let God in;
That is life, that's life.
God owns our lives,
Live your life to please Him only,
Live your life to please Him always,
For this brief life is not worth wasting.

10. Understanding Life

I took a walk up the road,
Saw different scenes of old,
Took the stroll with patient strides,
To explore the world all around.
The birds in the sky,
And sunset time,
Made it pleasant for exploration time.
Summer seems to fade,
And then I understood,
Life is not in the materialism it holds.
Life is in the love we share,
The good memories we create,
In the blessedness of God's gifts and love.

WHAT IS LOVE?

1. Let it go

Let it go, let it all go;
Let all the pains and aches all out,
Let it go, let it all go.
You need to go!
That is why you must let it go.
You need to move on,
If truly, then you must let go.
Let it go, let it go.
Let all the mistakes of the past be bygones,
Let it go, let it all go.
If love must continue greatly,
Move on by letting all go,
Let it go, let it go.

2. Let it go (II)

Let it go, let it all out,
Let all the pains be laid all out.
Let it go, let it all go.
If you look through the pane of the pains,

You'll never find any gain,
So let it go, let it all go.
Let it truly be bygones,
Apologize, say the I'm sorry word,
Forgive and let it truly be forgotten,
Let it go, let it go.

3. Family

For some days away to the east,
All alone after I finished the deals,
I lay on my bed to rest,
And my mind went to those I love.
Forgetting all that was there, I thought,
Of memories of wondrous love and fun,
Remembering all of whom I cherish,
Not just by blood but through love and bond.
I took my "mobile device" to explore more,
Of memories of wondrous love and fun,
And my heart melted and became warm,
At the amazing scenes of each story.
Unceasing, never stopping, I kept scrolling,
Boundlessly to the in-depths stories,
My emotions became emotional,
And in one instance, money became vanity.
Overwhelmed by memories, I realized family,
Friends, relatives and other colleagues,
And all those I could call homies,
Blessed family, blessed family I long to see.

4. My Mother

She was there when I needed her
She watched me grow
She warned me always

And wanted the best for me
She washed my head when I was ill
And my clothes does she wash also
She tells me of the future untold
The dreams that never should last, and in prayer, should I commit myself
She blesses and does not curse
She's like the pretty moonlight
That lights the moonlight flower
And day after day of every night
I think of how wonderful my mother had been.

5. Will you Still Love Me?

Shackled, will you still love me?
Weakened, will you still love me?
In pain, will you still love me?
Will you love me,
If I have nothing to give you?
Will you love me,
Just beyond what has been said?
Without pretense,
Will you still love me?
Will you love me to the end?

6. What is Love?

In her eyes, I knew,
She held me close with good,
She kissed me as I laid down me to rest,
And it felt so good, like the honeycomb.
What is Love?
It is a sacred bond.
It is one thing that calls you,
To leave all and accept "one".

7. Warnings to 21st-century Parents

A whole new world,
Yet it's filled with broken words.
New techs with fresh bonds,
But we forget the real ones.
Our children are losing us,
Because we seek a lifestyle that breaks us.
Work, work, work, more money and other stuff,
Yet it's never enough.
Time with us, they are losing all,
Why don't we go back to real love?
Truth be told, they really need us,
Parents reason now and spend time with the real ones.

8. Darkness in the Soul

Faked it too long, and now it's all wrong,
The trends was so full it dimmed us.
Dark deeds from it's seed that broke us,
See now these things that destroys.
Hate and distrust are moving up,
These dark things are bitter swords.
Freedom comes when we let love,
For only light and love can cure us.

9. Walls

Walls of old,
Cold and bold,
Pains and yokes,
Are the walls you hold.
Things of old,
That breaks and does not hold,
Is all you hold,
In the walls that you mould.

Many things of old,
But right here, right now,
Let down the walls....
And find peace, and let LOVE in.

10. In The Moon's Light

In the moon's light, on a certain night,
The moonlight shining bright rhymes with the night.
It was blooming and beaming good light that lovely night,
For that certain night was so effective for the light.
And then I saw, I was moved,
At such beauty of the crescent moonlight;
That bloomed goodness and love,
In the perfectness of God's true light.

VIRTUES

1. Dancing Rasta

Rasta, whose name was also called Pasta, rode on his coaster;
He rode his roller coaster skate along the "coast of plaster",
And as he rode, he danced and ended up in a crash.
Next, he was in the hospital with a lot of plasters,
And when his brother arrived, he said in pidgin, "he don start";
Are you a dancing Rasta?

2. Dancing Rasta (2)

His brother shouted again!
Do you think you can buy a canvas or a sandal with some cantas?
Or do they get the coins from the corn?
Rasta, his brother, said solemnly,
You are not dancing Rasta,
Are you?

3. I Miss The Rain

In the rain
In the puddles

Bathing endlessly
Running endlessly
Wishing endlessly
That the loving moments
Spent in the rain
Should not end
But it was not so
For dryness came
And made all dry
And its dry season
Caused everywhere
To be dusty
But I had hope
That one day, someday,
The rain will come again
And there will be laughter
And there will be joy
For a time to plant has come
And my wish to see rain again is fulfilled
Because, I miss the rain.

4. Trends (By Godly poems Ft. Theophy IP)

Top class and first rides,
Cozy bars and fresh lines,
Cruising on a king's cruise,
Nothing but all for the trends.
Love wasn't there,
The riches were fake,
And I was stunned by it's emptiness,
Nothing but all for the trends.
Nothing in my hands I bring, simply to thy Cross I cling...
Crossover — trends, paving more room for more crossroads...
Demeaned is the life, rewarded in strife in the land of woe.
Wonder is to yonder near grace...

Grace to live; greater to abide; thitherto!
JESUS is, to me, the bedrock of my salvation; salvaging.
The overturn of my true crime with no dime...
Just pay the noble price of obedience unto divine repentance, to be accepted in thy holy sanctuary...
Come one — deny none; the way of trends in thy ways!
Trend will stress,
Those who have ridden on its wings have been stressed.
You cannot all the time always trend,
It's pure fact, and it is dense.
The worldly dress, things and feels cannot stand in life's tests,
So seek the heavenly things that's beyond trends.
© Theophy IP
© Godly poems

5. Love and gratitude

Thankful for all,
Grateful to God,
The blessings are many,
I've counted them one by one.
What manner of love is this?
That leaves all to seek one;
An unbreakable bond it is,
That, surely, I'm grateful for.

6. Immersion

Into the fountain, cleansing deep,
Into the newness of hope and dream,
A new heart and mind all anew,
To see the visions and untold truth.
Immersion....., into the deep things I went,
Renewed so I could run with the visions of truth,
Decisions at many crossroads are there,

But I 'immersed' now understand the way of truth.
What is seen is not all that is true,
If you seek what's real, you'll find out the truth,
Immersion, change for the soul brand new,
He that hath an ear, let him hear what is true.
The journey is not how swift or quick,
But in the hope that qualifies, that redeems.
The other side of the beat is the beat rhythm,
The other side of the coin is not a corn.
Immersion...., this is Life's real direction.
That you seek the path of worthy ambition,
- the great versions for your dimensions,
And avoid the diversions route to perversions.

7. Meekness

Meekness is not 'milk-ness',
Meekness reflects gentleness.
Meekness of the mind with the heart,
It seeks peace and finds peace,
Being meek comes with God's grace,
For the meekness of heart gentles your spirit.

8. Old and wise

Cold as ice,
Young and smart.
Wild we've become,
Because we failed to be wise.
Seeking the fakes,
And living in lust,
Pushing the limits,
Yet breaking every trust.
Old and wise,
Who is a wise man?

He's one who fights to see peace.
Not with his fists,
But repairing the broken things,
And this is not a mist.
Wisdom comes from above,
And as we grow old,
Learn from the wrongs of old,
Seek to do right and be wise.

9. The Wisdom Of Time

Time is life; in it, there's a timeline.
It is universally non-reversible,
Cause it never depends on anybody's work time.
Time is life; in it, there's a lifetime,
Be wise, use thy given time and live right.
Open your eyes, be not unwise,
Cause unused time has its prize.

10. The Rising Sun

Another day is here,
As the rising sun sets.
The better days are near,
Rise up and do not fear.
Look up and see the bright sky,
See how it's cleared,
Up above the sun is there,
The rising sun has set.

TOMORROW AND BEYOND

1. Eternity

Longer than time it is,
The lifespan of our
never-dying God.
It's days are elaborate
and out of numbers.
It has no ending,
for it is not timed.
Oh Eternity, Oh Eternity,
You're closer than ever.
This is my desire and prayer,
That I spend my eternity in Heaven
with God my Father.

2. Time

Time, thy wonders of events is numerous,
Thy nature is of God,
But thy characteristics was discovered by man.
At thy sound and start do things happen.
You're a substance to be treasured,
You are independent of everything,
You separate events from events,

And only God can stop you.

3. New things

New things come every day,
New things reflect the old,
New things build strongly.
I saw a man with a new thing,
I saw this man who I knew before,
For he has now a new heart.
"New things come, new things go",
But what do you do with every new thing God gives you?

4. The Old Soldier Walks Home

Bouncing in style, he walks,
In humility, he bows,
To those he had long seen.
Walking and waving,
He sees the long-time story of many things.
And while he walked,
He saw laughter in the hearts of many,
All along the way.
Till he got home,
Wonders of change glared into his eyes,
And beautiful was each story.
Finally, he got home,
At the stairway, he stopped,
And read to himself a sign-
The old soldier comes home
And with a smile,
He entered to see those he loves.

5. Consequences

You cannot choose the path of GUNS and expect not to see the GUNS,
You cannot advise someone in toxic love,
Many times, they're always the last ones to know.
You cannot swear an oath and say you don't know,
consequences.........., they will surely show.
Loving money above God, the end result is that money cannot save any from God's wrath.
Consequences.........!! they will surely show!
You reap what you sow, and whatsoever you sow, you will surely reap;
This is the ancient law - the ancient law of sowing and reaping.
You cannot hide the consequences of the sins,
You cannot bride it not to show!
Consequences......, It will surely show!
You say it's all in the past, but God requires the past,
So you better go make peace with your past,
Or else your sins' consequences will destroy your peace.
Repentance is key- you must repent of your sins,
Don't hide the deeds of evil things, for "consequences don't sleep".
Even hand joined in hand, the wicked shall not go unpunished,
So live right, do it right, make peace with thy past,
And walk always in the way that pleases God with all your heart.

6. Hopeless Hope

Sinner man in sin,
Wants to continue in sin,
To the end, living in pleasures of sin,
And wants to arrive in Heaven for real.
"Heaven laughs at this dream",
For this hope is a hopeless hope.
The way of hope is the narrow road,
Oh sinner man, repent of your sins!

There's a way that seems right unto a man,
But the end is destruction, despair and tears.
Oh sinner man, run to Jesus today!
He is the only hope for this world of sin,
Run to Him, and be saved from your sins.

7. Plans

Plans are plans,
Plans, plans are just plans.
Plans may be secret,
Plans may be open,
Plans, plans are just plans.
Plan is one letter short of plane,
For thy plans should be plain,
Plans, plans are just plans.
Planning with purpose reflects God,
For when we plan our life in God,
We are free to open more of our plans to Him.

8. Commitment

He said later, but was late as ever.
Coming back, you said I will but doeth not.
Commitment that faileth, is poor of trust.
Commitment to good love brings faith,
And when you trust one another,
Commitment keeps you one to another.

9. My Thoughts and I

I've been thinking of the thoughtful things,
Deep thoughts of great promising feels,
Thinking thoughts that have deepened my mind,
My heart and soul has lost track of time.
Scenery was each different imagination,

Hmm...., what shall I do with these thinking thoughts?
I took a step further, my thoughts and I,
To let go of these thinking thoughts and act.
Thinking is just thinking, it doesn't really solve what 'tinks',
If you stay too long, you lose track of the 'tick tick',
So wake up to the real things, move on with the big dreams,
And apply actions to those 'thoughtful dreams'.

10. Cadre of Civilization

The increase in population,
Has brought people's association;
With communication and information,
The foundation of civilization was formed.

NOT THAT WAY

1. Drifting drift

In seeking more, he's losing all,
He's 'chasing clouds' with no silver lining,
Prodigal-like is now his cruising-like,
Drifting drift, like the car drift, has drifted too far.
Gone from the way, far from the path-
His eyes are now filled with things that blind,
He walks no more in righteousness,
Drifting drift, now walks in the dirt-death path.
Hope for the blind, is there any hope for the prodigal?
Repentance and sincere turning away from that sinful way!
Oh saved man, drift no more, stand always for Christ,
The way of the cross leads HOME.

2. Does the Law transgress? (By Godly Poems ft. Nicky Inks)

Does the law transgress?
Does the law breed lies?
To deny the access of a free man
Is nothing but making the law transgress

Does the law transgress?
Does the sacred hand of law engage in unholy acts of avarice and greed?
Does the law transgress?
Does the law sacrifice justice on the marble altar of silence for the sake of peace?
They say the law is blind.
Is it also blind to the cries of pain?
Does the law transgress?
Is the law law-abiding?
To hide the truth in the law
Is nothing but making the law transgress
© Godly Poems ft. Nicky Inks Collins Otuoze Thomas

3. DRUMS (Drugs & Alcohol Abuse)

Dooms and glums lie in the rums and drugs. Unstable drums these are, causing itching and sinking sight to man.
Addictions and possessions follow these drums,
Binding they can be, if you loose the door and let them in.
Drugs and alcohol abuse - pleasures that yoke,
Freedom and law backing these all - blurs the more.
Listen to the words of the wise and flee
worldly lusts,
Also, alcohol and drugs and those dimmers that breed bonds.

4. Fantasy real

The fake became original,
The original became fake.
The trends of fantasy blues,
And fake goods became the rules.
The origin seems broken,
Cause fake things,
Now blind the real "goods."

5. Sleeping Giants

Sleeping giant, awake from thy slumber,
Be not blind to what really matters,
Oh sleeping giant awake and arise.
How long will thou lumber in thy slumber?
Don't you see the days are numbered?
Oh sleeping giant, awake! Awake and rise! Awake and conquer!
Justice has fallen under thy watch,
And thou does not bother,
Who has bewitched thee that thou can't see what really matters?
Oh sleeping giant, awake! from 'this slumber',
Linger not, or else thou shall be outnumbered,
Repent now! Arise and fight-fight for what truly matters!

6. Seriously Unserious

If I told you and showed you the way, will you walk therein?
Or will you look for another that isn't, just so you can blend in?
You speak of doing, but you do not.
You wish all, but you try not.
Seriously unserious, you're too unserious,
Jokingly serious, you're always losing focus!
You think you know all, but you can't even get one.
You're swayed away, and you think that's the way?
Are you serious? Are you sure you are?
Then why can't you focus and get this done?
I laugh in an uncommon culture because,
You don't even know where you are driving to as you drive!
You shout and spark, but your record is still zero-score!
Seriously......?
This is unbelievable and seriously unserious.
You drive in circles because the way is blurred to your eyes.
Your life is undefined because you're living in fantasy lies.
How much help have you gotten? Yet none has proved bright.
Always waiting for time, when time gave you enough.

So sad and disheartening is this,
Awake now, be not unwise, turn around and become serious.

7. Lost in Lust

The mindset becomes dull,
The heart becomes blurred,
The imaginations- dimmed and lost;
It's all in the 'waste-lines' that breeds his lust.
Extreme passions in carnal desires fill his eyes,
In seeing he sees not - lost in life.
His feeling kills all, desiring more - bonds that tie,
Lost in time - Lost in lust.
Lost in that life, in the bonds that tie,
Is there a way to be free from a lustful life?
Open your eyes, run to Christ,
HE delivers and changes every life.

8. Whoredom

She's in a realm, She's out to destroy men,
Her ways lead to hell, for she's the daughter of Jezebel.
She dwells in a deep well -
It's her dark world full of lusts and bonds.
All types of men are on her list - the rich, the strong, and even the hustling ones.
She seeks them without remorse,
Like a ravening beast killing a young one.
Carnal doors she opens to all, to all who come into her world!
She's stopping for none, for she has sworn to destroy to the very last one.
Oh righteous man, flee from lust!
Through her pleasures, she lures and allures,
Till she locks them in that scary world.
Sinful pleasures are her weapon to call,

To call all sorts and make them as broken cords.

9. Twisting Twists

Confusions they are, blinking lights and unstable waters,
Core deceivers with a mask of truth,
Here and there, deceiving many with false truth.
False teachers, false prophets, false ministers,
Walking as sheep but are hungry wolves.
These are twisting twists,
They have no stable ground because they are blinking lights.
Lies are in their heart, carnality in their mind and lust in their life.
Twisting twists have twisted many,
They curl it the way they want, they twist them the way they want!
Twisting twists are destroying holy things.
Politicians too are involved, the leaders at the top, some are strongly deceiving us!
It's all in the system, to control more,
Twisting twists, the dark power of this world- that's their tactic!
Don't forget, from the very beginning, it was deception that ruined it all.
So, run from it all and avoid their deception.

10. Twisting Twists 2

There are many walking lies in this modern time,
Transgender perversions and many other corruptions,
'They' say the man can go, that the woman with some science can be the man.
What a sad-dark, twisted twist.
Can a 'man-go' be a woman?
'They' say they will prove it with the 'law',
Twisted twist, even their law is twisted.
Love, many are seeking it wrongly because they've believed some twists,

The other side is telling them truthful lies,
And they have believed it with their whole heart.
You cannot find love there, you cannot find any love in twisted twists.
Can any be saved? one may ask,
The way of the CROSS is the only way that can save us all.
Return back to God! Return to thy saviour!
Deceptions cannot stand the light of God's truthful words,
The hopeful path from all these lies is to turn to the true God,
Through Christ Jesus His Son.

www.ingramcontent.com/pod-product-compliance
Lightning Source LLC
LaVergne TN
LVHW041238150826
845673LV00008B/2419